A Night at the Ballet

Stories of Great Ballets
with Late Elementary to Early Intermediate Piano Arrangements

Bernadine Johnson & Margaret Goldston

A Night at the Ballet takes piano students on a fascinating journey into the exciting world of ballet. The book presents stories and music from some of the most beloved ballets in history. Along with late-elementary to early-intermediate piano arrangements of favorite ballet themes, it includes instructions for organizing a ballet-themed recital, information on the basics of ballet, an explanation of ballet terms, highlights of ballet history and more.

Seven timeless ballets are explored. The section on each ballet includes:

- **a piano arrangement by Margaret Goldston of music from the ballet**
- **an easy-to-understand summary of the ballet's story**
- **interesting background information on the ballet**
- **a brief biography of the composer**
- **a fun activity page**

Table of Contents

To The Teacher

How to Create *A Night at the Ballet*

Instructions for Organizing a Ballet-Themed Recital

This book can be used to present a theme recital that combines piano performance with interesting information about the ballet repertoire that is featured. This can be a creative and fun way to involve students of all ages and ability levels from your studio.

Before the program

1. Choose the ballets to present from this book.
2. Assign everyone in your studio a specific duty: presenting background information, piano performance, handing out programs, welcoming guests to the recital, helping with publicity, refreshments, setup or cleanup.
3. Have a dress rehearsal at the performance facility so that the students become familiar with the piano, the microphone (if used), where to stand, etc.
4. Contact local newspapers for coverage of the event.

Optional ideas:

• Invite local dance students to perform dances to some of the selections. More advanced students could accompany the dancers. Be sure to invite any of your own piano students who study ballet to dance in the recital.

• Advanced students could present more difficult arrangements of ballet music (found at your local music store).

The program

1. Ask two students to dress as ballerinas and pass out programs at the door.
2. Have a recording of ballet music playing in the background as guests arrive.
3. Begin the program with some highlights of ballet history (see pages 12–13).
4. Present each ballet as follows: interesting facts about the ballet, the composer's biography, the story of the ballet, and the performance of the solo selection.
5. Encourage performers to "dress up" to give the evening a special elegance.

After the program

1. Serve refreshments that represent the ballets. (For example: swan cookies for *Swan Lake*, an assortment of nuts for *The Nutcracker*, French pastries or "white desserts" for *Les Sylphides*.)
2. Submit a videotape of the program to your local cable television station. (Check with the station to be sure you are not violating copyright laws.)

Ballet Basics

What is a ballet?

A ballet is a theatrical performance of solo and group dances performed to music, using a pattern of steps called "choreography." A ballet often tells a story.

What does the word "ballet" mean?

The word "ballet" means "to dance." "Ballet" is the French spelling of the Italian word "ballare."[1] The French language is used for teaching ballet.

What is classical ballet?

Classical ballet is a style of dance that follows the techniques developed in the 17th century by the *Académie Royale de Danse*, founded by King Louis XIV. The term also applies to ballets from the second half of the 19th century (such as *The Nutcracker*) in which pattern, movement and form are essential.

What kinds of dances are in a classical ballet?

Classical ballets usually include:
1. dances for the *corps de ballet*[2] (dancers who perform together in a group);
2. *variations* (solos with a series of difficult moves);
3. at least one *pas de deux*[3] (dance for two).

Classical ballet is based on what two important things?

1. *The turnout:* The dancer's legs and feet must be turned outward. This separates ballet from all other forms of theatrical dance.
2. *The five positions:* All moves start and end from these positions.

A pas de deux—a dance for two—from the ballet Coppélia

---

[1] pronounced "bahl-LAH-ray"

[2] pronounced "core de bal-LAY"

[3] pronounced "pah deh deuh"

What Are the Five Positions?

ARM POSITIONS

FOOT POSITIONS

The poem and illustrations below will help you understand the five positions.

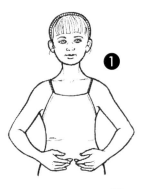

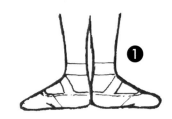

Positions are a special way
To place the arms and feet,
And when the head and hands are placed,
The picture is complete.

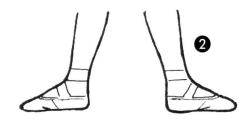

Positions are the first thing
That a dancer has to learn;
It's how they start and end each move
And balance every turn.

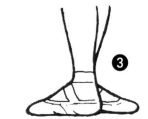

Positions were created
'Bout five hundred years ago.
A teacher named Pierre Beauchamps[1]
Thought they'd be good to know.

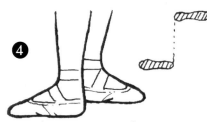

Fourth Position, Opened

Pierre was ballet master
For Louis,[2] the King of France.
He borrowed moves from fencing[3]
And he used them to teach dance.

Five positions for the feet
And five for arms, as well;
They must be practiced 'til they feel
Completely "naturale."

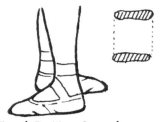

Fourth Position, Crossed

The five positions are the moves
All students must obey.
They are the basic alphabet
For all who dance ballet!

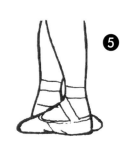

[1] pronounced "pee-AYR boo-SHAWM"

[2] pronounced "loo-EE"

[3] Fencing is sword-fighting.

Studying Ballet Today

Ballet dancers are the same all over the world. They wear the same clothes in the dance studio and practice the same steps, often in the same order.

Learning to dance is hard work. Dancers usually appear in the *corps de ballet* during their early years. As a dancer gains experience, he or she plays more important roles until finally becoming a soloist. Only the very best female dancers are called *ballerinas*.

What do you need to be a good dancer?

You need to
1. be strong,
2. have good coordination,
3. be able to jump,
4. have good turnout,
5. have the strength to lift your legs easily.

How often do dancers practice?

Dancers never stop studying. They return to the classroom every day to practice and keep in shape.

What happens during ballet class?

Class begins with exercises at the *barre*,[1] a wooden rail attached to the studio wall. This is followed by floor exercises in the middle of the room. Mirrors in the room help students correct their positions.

Is talking allowed during class?

Silence is required during class. The dressing room is where students change clothes and talk to their friends.

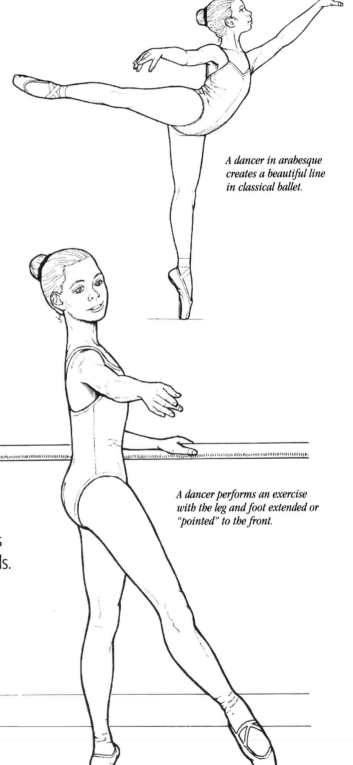

A dancer in arabesque creates a beautiful line in classical ballet.

A dancer performs an exercise with the leg and foot extended or "pointed" to the front.

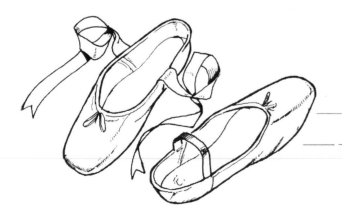

[1] pronounced "bar"

What does the teacher do during class?

The teacher moves around the room correcting positions and giving advice.

Is there anything special that girls learn?

Girls have to learn how to dance on their toes. Dancing on the tips of the toes is called *en pointe*.[1]

When do girls begin to wear pointe shoes?

Female dancers do not use pointe shoes until the teacher decides that the ankles, back and supporting muscles are strong enough (usually around age 13).

How do girls dress for dance class?

Girls wear leotards, tights and ballet slippers. Their hair is pulled back and pinned neatly to the head so that the neck can be easily seen. No jewelry is allowed.

Pointe shoes are made with layers of hardened glue and cloth. The shoes have a thin, flexible leather sole to give support.

Is there anything special that boys learn?

Boys learn to lift girls into the air.

What do boys wear for dance class?

Boys wear a white t-shirt, black tights and ballet slippers. They must keep their hair short.

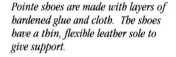

Stretching the back of the leg is part of a ballerina's warm up.

---

[1] pronounced "ahn point"

The History of Ballet (in Song)

The melodies that follow are taken from ballets that you will study later in this book. The words to the melodies answer questions that relate to the history of ballet.

Practice directions: • First, play the melody with the correct fingerings.
• Then sing the words as you play the melody.

Where does the word "ballet" come from?

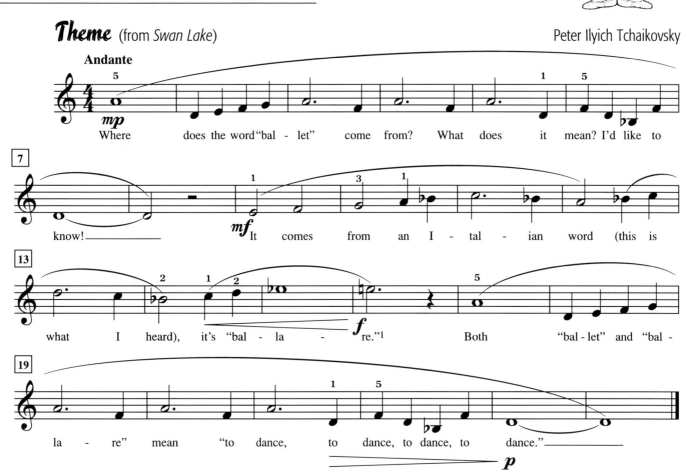

Theme (from *Swan Lake*)   Peter Ilyich Tchaikovsky

Where does the word "bal - let" come from? What does it mean? I'd like to

know!_____ It comes from an I - tal - ian word (this is

what I heard), it's "bal - la - re."[1] Both "bal - let" and "bal -

la - re" mean "to dance, to dance, to dance, to dance."_____

Where was the first ballet school?

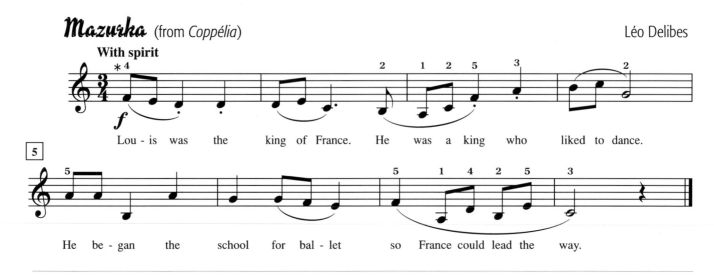

Mazurka (from *Coppélia*)   Léo Delibes

Lou - is was the king of France. He was a king who liked to dance.

He be - gan the school for bal - let so France could lead the way.

---

[1] pronounced "bahl-LAH-ray"

*Throughout the piece, ♩ ♩ can be played as ♩. ♪ as originally written by Delibes.

What language is used for ballet?

Waltz (from *The Sleeping Beauty*)

Peter Ilyich Tchaikovsky

Please speak French be - cause it's the lan - guage of bal -

let;_____ that's be - cause the ve - ry first school to teach bal -

let was in France. So say, "É - chap - pé and pas de deux,

re - le - vé, je - té."[1]_____ These are_____ some

French words_____ we use in_____ bal - let._____

What are the female and male ballet dancers called?

Can-Can (from *Gaîté Parisienne*)

Jacques Offenbach

A "bal - le - ri - na" is a fe - male and a

male is called a "dan - seur"[1] or some - times a "bal - le - ri - no."

At first the dan - cers were all men be - cause it

was - n't "la - dy - like" for girls to dance on stage.

[1] See glossary (page 56) for pronunciation of these words.

Who was Marie Camargo?

Dance of the Sugarplum Fairy (from *The Nutcracker*)

Peter Ilyich Tchaikovsky

Bal-le - ri - na Ma - rie Ca-mar-go, long a - go said, "Oh - oh! I need short-er skirts

so the peo - ple watch - ing see my feet (what a treat). Now I'll jump and I won't get hurt."

It was al - so Ma - rie Ca-mar-go, long a - go said, "Oh-oh! I need flat-ter shoes.

Then I'll jump high on my first try 'cause of the shoes that I use!"

Who was Marie Taglioni¹?

Dance of the Hours (from *La Gioconda*)

Amilcare Ponchielli

Miss Ta-glio-ni, Miss Ta-glio-ni, it was dan-cer Miss Ta-glio-ni, who first

danced on all her tip-toes, the first one to go "en pointe." Now all the world knows. She in -

vent-ed some leg warm-ers. They're a big help to per - form-ers. She cut

sleeves off of a sweat-er; put them on her legs so that they would feel bet-ter.

¹ pronounced "tah-LYOH-nee"

What important contribution did Jean Georges¹ Noverre make to ballet?

Grand Waltz *(from Les Sylphides)* — Frédéric François Chopin

Lyrics:

Please use some mime, please use your face when danc-ing bal - let. There's a sto - ry to tell; to do it well you need to use all of your-self. This new i-dea came from the man Jean Georges— from France. He be-lieved it would be help-ful to see some act-ing with dance. Hope you sang a-long on this his-t'ry song a - bout bal - let.

¹ pronounced "zhahn zhorzh"

Highlights of Ballet History

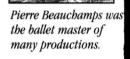

1400s–1500s

- Domenico da Piacenza (Italy) writes the first important paper on dancing by notating how dance steps were to be performed.

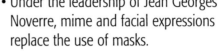

- In the courts of European royalty, "masques" become popular. Performers wore masks and entertained with poetry, singing, dancing and beautiful costumes.

Masked male dancer

- Italian violinist Baldassarino de Belgiojoso presents the first ballet, *Ballet Comique de la Reine*, uniting Italian opera and French dance.

- The first book on dancing, *Orchesographie* by Thoinot Arbeau, is published in France.

1600s

- King Louis XIV of France opens the first ballet school, the *Académie Royale de Danse* (1661).

- Jean-Baptiste Lully, an important composer in the court of Louis XIV, assists in introducing ballet as a regular part of opera and creates dances that are complex in pattern and floor design.

- Lully's ballet, *The Triumph of Love*, premieres in Paris (1681). This is the first ballet to use female dancers. Men continue to dance female roles (wearing masks) until there are enough trained women dancers.

1700s

- Pierre Beauchamps, choreographer and first ballet master of the *Académie*, develops the five basic positions.

- A systematic training method for ballet dancers is created.

- Under the leadership of Jean Georges Noverre, mime and facial expressions replace the use of masks.

Pierre Beauchamps was the ballet master of many productions.

- Ballet becomes more theatrical and female dancers become more technical, using leaps and difficult footwork.

- Ballerina Marie Camargo is the first to shorten her skirts so the public can see her footwork.

- Flat, flexible slippers are developed, allowing for new technical skills.

- *Ballet d'action* (ballet that tells a complete story) is developed.

- Ballet is still included in opera, but it also becomes a form of entertainment itself.

A ballet d'action, expresses in steps, gestures and movement what is difficult to say in words.

Timeline of Important Events in Ballet History

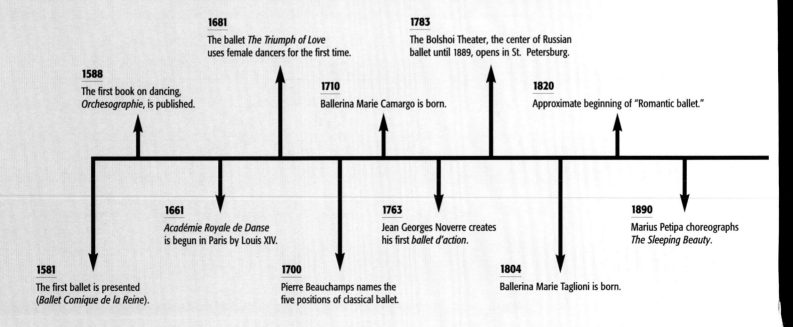

1588 The first book on dancing, *Orchesographie*, is published.

1681 The ballet *The Triumph of Love* uses female dancers for the first time.

1710 Ballerina Marie Camargo is born.

1783 The Bolshoi Theater, the center of Russian ballet until 1889, opens in St. Petersburg.

1820 Approximate beginning of "Romantic ballet."

1581 The first ballet is presented (*Ballet Comique de la Reine*).

1661 *Académie Royale de Danse* is begun in Paris by Louis XIV.

1700 Pierre Beauchamps names the five positions of classical ballet.

1763 Jean Georges Noverre creates his first *ballet d'action*.

1804 Ballerina Marie Taglioni is born.

1890 Marius Petipa choreographs *The Sleeping Beauty*.

1800s

- "Classical ballet" (a style with a strict technique) reaches its height.

- "Romantic ballet" develops, emphasizing strong emotions (such as love, death and anger), with supernatural stories (involving magic, spirits, etc.).

Giselle is an example of a romantic ballet.

- The pointe shoe is created. Ballerinas, led by Marie Taglioni, begin to dance *en pointe* (on tiptoe).

- Female dancers become more popular than male dancers.

- Choreographer Marius Petipa takes control of Russian ballet, stressing classical technique and the importance of music and stage effects.

- French ballet declines in popularity as Russian ballet becomes more popular. Russian ballet greatly influences classical ballet from the late 1800s throughout the 1900s.

- Russian composer Peter Ilyich Tchaikovsky wrote the music for his three ballets (*The Sleeping Beauty*, *The Nutcracker* and *Swan Lake*).

1900–present

- Russian director Serge Diaghilev combines the best dancers, choreographers, writers, composers and set designers to create the famous classical ballet company, the *Ballet Russes*. This company included the famous dancers Anna Pavlova and Vaslav Nijinsky.

Vaslav Nijinsky in Petrouchka

- Choreographer Michel Fokine helps make the Diaghilev ballets revolutionary for their time. His masterpieces include *Les Sylphides*, *Petrushka*, and *The Firebird*.

- Modern dance develops, mostly as a result of American contributions.

- George Balanchine, one of the greatest choreographers in ballet history, creates ballets that are danced by many companies.

- Choreographer Robert Joffrey establishes his own company, The Joffrey Ballet (1952).

- Ballet technique becomes an important part of the Broadway musical with the contributions of choreographers Agnes de Mille (*Oklahoma, Carousel, Brigadoon*) and Jerome Robbins (*West Side Story, The King and I, Fiddler on the Roof*).

- Russian dancers begin defecting to the West. Among them are Rudolf Nureyev (1961), Mikhail Baryshnikov (1974) and Alexander Godunov (1979).

- Choreographer Twyla Tharp invents a new method of dancing by using, but changing, elements of popular dance with the speed and precision of ballet technique.

- The study of ballet becomes an important aspect of training for figure skaters and other athletes.

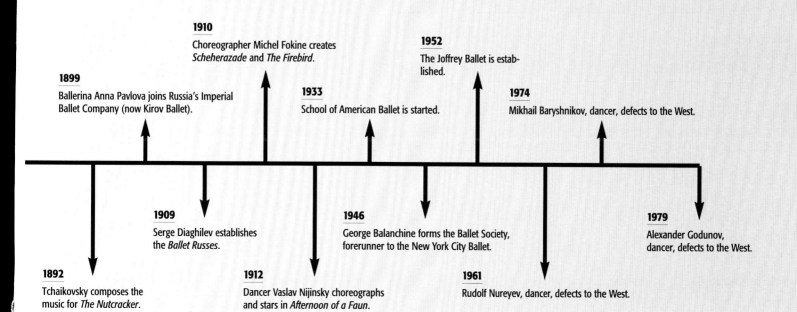

1899 Ballerina Anna Pavlova joins Russia's Imperial Ballet Company (now Kirov Ballet).

1910 Choreographer Michel Fokine creates *Scheherazade* and *The Firebird*.

1933 School of American Ballet is started.

1952 The Joffrey Ballet is established.

1974 Mikhail Baryshnikov, dancer, defects to the West.

1892 Tchaikovsky composes the music for *The Nutcracker*.

1909 Serge Diaghilev establishes the *Ballet Russes*.

1912 Dancer Vaslav Nijinsky choreographs and stars in *Afternoon of a Faun*.

1946 George Balanchine forms the Ballet Society, forerunner to the New York City Ballet.

1961 Rudolf Nureyev, dancer, defects to the West.

1979 Alexander Godunov, dancer, defects to the West.

Swan Lake

A Dramatic Ballet in Four Acts

Composer: **Peter Ilyich Tchaikovsky**

Story: **Based on a German folk tale**

First performed: **1877 in Moscow, Russia**

The Story

It is Prince Siegfried's 21st birthday, and the townspeople have been invited to the castle to celebrate with refreshments and dancing. It is the custom of the time for a prince to choose a wife when he turns 21. The prince's mother tells him that she has planned a ball for the next evening. She has invited eligible young ladies so the prince can choose a wife to share the throne with him. Siegfried protests, saying that he is not ready to get married because he is not in love. His mother says that this does not matter, and he will have to select a wife at the ball.

That night, Siegfried and his friends go hunting. He sees some swans on a lake and takes aim with his bow. Suddenly, the swans change into beautiful girls. Odette, the Swan Queen, tells Siegfried that an evil sorcerer named Rothbart cast a spell that turned them into swans, only returning them to human form between midnight and dawn. The only way Odette's spell can be broken is for someone to promise to marry her and swear he will never pledge his love for anyone else. Siegfried, who has fallen in love with Odette at first sight, promises to marry her. They are unaware that Rothbart is hiding nearby and listening.

The following evening, the castle is filled with guests and entertainers in their finest clothes, enjoying the food, dancing and entertainment at the birthday ball. Rothbart arrives in disguise along with his daughter, Odile, who has been magically changed to look like Odette. Siegfried, thinking she is Odette, pledges his love for her in front of everyone and agrees to marry her. He does not see the real Odette outside the castle window, wildly flapping her wings in warning. Rothbart reveals that he has tricked the prince and that Siegfried will never be able to be with his true love.

When Siegfried realizes his mistake, he rushes to the lake to find Odette and explain. Odette, now in human form, forgives him. She decides that she will not live as a swan the rest of her life and belong to Rothbart. She kisses Siegfried one last time and jumps into the lake to die. Siegfried, not wanting to live without her, follows her into the lake so they can be together in death. The power of their love destroys Rothbart and his magic. As Rothbart dies, all the swans are released from his evil magic, and Siegfried and Odette are united forever in the afterlife.

About the Ballet

Swan Lake, Tchaikovsky's first ballet, began as a play for his nieces and nephews to perform for the family. He later turned it into a full-length ballet when he was asked to write for the Bolshoi Theater in Moscow. *Swan Lake* is a four-act ballet based on a German folk tale. Unfortunately, the ballet was a failure when it was first performed, partly due to poor choreography and stage decoration. In 1895, new choreography was created, and the ballet became an immediate success. Sadly, Tchaikovsky died two years before, thinking that the ballet was a failure. It is now one of the most popular ballets in the world.

All leading ballerinas hope to dance in *Swan Lake* during their careers. The roles of Odette (dressed as a white swan) and the evil Odile (dressed as a black swan) are usually danced by the same ballerina. The choreography contains many difficult steps for both the female and male lead dancers. *Cygnets*, the French word for "little swans," is the title of a famous dance number from the ballet. Four of the smallest dancers perform this dance.

About the Composer

Peter Ilyich Tchaikovsky (1840–1893) was born in Russia. At age four he wrote his first musical composition, then began piano lessons when he was seven years old.

In addition to becoming a world-famous composer, Tchaikovsky was also a great conductor, teacher of composition and music critic. He was the first composer to treat ballet music as serious orchestral music, believing that the music is as important as the dancing. Tchaikovsky's three ballets (*Swan Lake*, *The Sleeping Beauty* and *The Nutcracker*) are still favorites all over the world.

About the Music: Theme (arrangement on pages 18–19)

The *Theme* from *Swan Lake* is the ballet's most familiar music and is heard throughout the performance. It is a sad, mournful melody when first performed by the oboe at the opening of the ballet, then takes on a stronger, more frightening sound when later played by the trombones.

Swan Lake Word Search

*Using the list at the bottom of the page, look down,
across and diagonally to find the words hidden in the puzzle.
Circle the words.*

```
P C Y G N E T S D F K A H Y
R R N W O T Y F X R O T U S
L L I A D N H U N T I N G L
S W A N Q U E E N Z R T I M
O P H B C E L G M D R I S U
R O E I M E U J A E O P L Z
C E M L T O S A C R T C W R
E N G S L E B I R T H D A Y
R S Q U A Z C H G E B I O S
E T W E K B D E T F A N D O
R C A I E L F M C W R L I R
U E X T B A L L H E T I L D
L P R O N C B O D E T T E K
T C H A I K O V S K Y J M D
```

PRINCE	**ODETTE**
TCHAIKOVSKY	**SORCERER**
ROTHBART	**HUNTING**
SWAN QUEEN	**LAKE**
BIRTHDAY	**ODILE**
CYGNETS	**BALL**

Swan position from Swan Lake

Theme

(from *Swan Lake*)

Peter Ilyich Tchaikovsky
Arr. Margaret Goldston

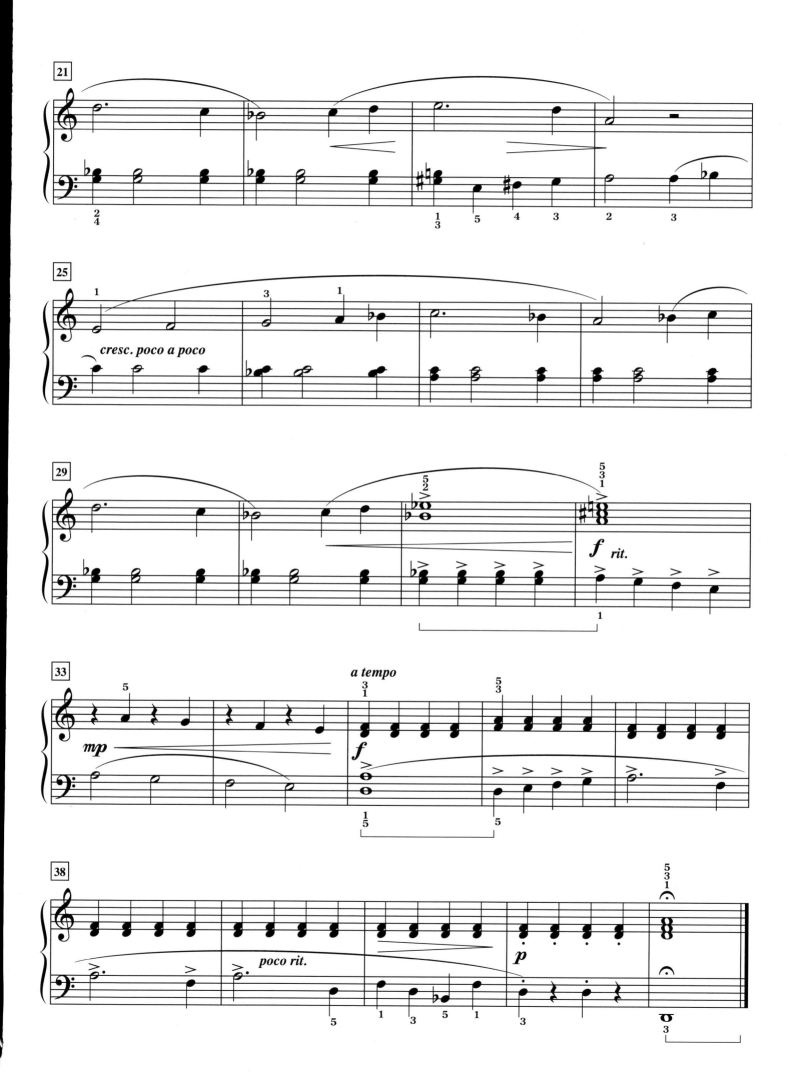

The Sleeping Beauty

A Dramatic Ballet in Three Acts

Composer: **Peter Ilyich Tchaikovsky**

Story: **Based on a French fairy tale by Charles Perrault**

First performed: **1890 in St. Petersburg, Russia**

The Story

It is the royal christening of the newborn princess Aurora. Her parents, the king and queen, invite many of the fairies from the kingdom to attend. While presents are being given to the royal family, the evil fairy Carabosse appears. She tells the king and queen how angry she is for not being invited. As her revenge, she puts an evil curse on Princess Aurora. One day Aurora will prick her finger on something sharp and die. The queen begs Carabosse to change her mind, but the evil fairy only laughs.

Fortunately, the good Lilac Fairy still has her gift to give the royal family. Although she cannot take away the curse, she can change it. The princess will not die, but instead she will fall into a deep sleep. Only the kiss of a handsome prince can wake her and break the spell. The king, trying to protect the princess, banishes all sharp objects from the palace.

The years pass. On Aurora's 16th birthday, her friends all gather in the palace gardens to celebrate with dancing. Four handsome princes have traveled from other kingdoms, hoping to marry Aurora. They each dance with the princess and offer her a rose as proof of their love. The evil Carabosse, disguised as an old woman joining the celebration, gives Aurora a bouquet of flowers with a needle hidden inside. While dancing with the flowers, Aurora pricks her finger and falls to the ground. As Carabosse disappears in a flash of lightning, the Lilac Fairy appears and suggests that the sleeping princess be carried into the castle. She waves her hand and a magic forest of vines grows around the castle, casting a spell of sleep over everyone inside.

One hundred years later, a handsome prince is hunting in a forest near the castle. The Lilac Fairy magically appears and reveals a vision of the sleeping Princess Aurora to him. He falls in love with her at first sight. The Lilac Fairy leads him through the thick forest to the castle where Aurora lies sleeping. When the prince kisses her, she awakens. They declare their love for each other and decide to marry. Everyone in the castle slowly awakens and begins to make preparations for the royal wedding.

Princess Aurora from
The Sleeping Beauty

Designs for
The Sleeping Beauty *costumes*

About the Ballet

The Sleeping Beauty is Tchaikovsky's second ballet, written 13 years after *Swan Lake*. It is based on a French fairy tale by Charles Perrault that was first published in 1697. Tchaikovsky wrote a complete outline of the ballet in only 40 days. Later, he worked very carefully with the choreographer to match every note he wrote with each dance step that was created. Because many people thought that the dancing was the most important part of a ballet, Tchaikovsky was determined to make his ballet music as important as the music was for an opera or a symphony.

One of the delightful features of *The Sleeping Beauty* is that other fairy-tale characters join the court to celebrate the marriage of Aurora and the prince at the end of the ballet. Aurora introduces these characters as her childhood friends. The characters change with different productions of the ballet, but may include Goldilocks, Beauty and the Beast, and Little Red Riding Hood.

About the Composer

Peter Ilyich Tchaikovsky (1840–1893) is one of the most well-known Russian composers. Because of his ballets and orchestral music, he was the first Russian composer to attain world-wide popularity. One of his most famous orchestral compositions is the *1812 Overture* which uses real cannons at the end of the piece. His last work was his *Symphony No. 6*. Tchaikovsky died soon after its first performance, and it was played at his funeral service.

After seeing Tchaikovsky's *The Sleeping Beauty*, Sergei Prokofiev and Igor Stravinsky (two great Russian composers of ballet music) both knew that someday they wanted to write ballets.

About the Music: Waltz (arrangement on pages 24–25)

The *Waltz* from *The Sleeping Beauty* is performed in the first act, with 16 couples dancing to celebrate Princess Aurora's 16th birthday.

In 1959, Walt Disney's animated feature *Sleeping Beauty* came to movie theaters. Disney hired composer George Bruns to adapt Tchaikovsky's classic music for use in the movie. The movie's famous song, *Once upon a Dream,* uses the music from Tchaikovsky's waltz.

The Sleeping Beauty

Fill in the blanks using the list of words at the bottom of the page.

1. _____ is the composer of *The Sleeping Beauty*.

2. *The Sleeping Beauty* is the composer's _____ ballet.

3. It is the story of a princess named _____ .

4. Carabosse, the _____ fairy, puts a curse on the baby princess.

5. The Lilac Fairy changes the curse from death to _____ .

6. On her _____ birthday, the princess pricks her finger.

7. The entire castle falls asleep for _____ years.

8. A handsome _____ rescues the sleeping princess.

9. The princess is awakened with a _____ .

EVIL	**PRINCE**
ONE HUNDRED	**16TH**
TCHAIKOVSKY	**AURORA**
KISS	**SLEEP**
SECOND	

Waltz

(from *The Sleeping Beauty*)

Peter Ilyich Tchaikovsky
Arr. Margaret Goldston

Tempo di valse

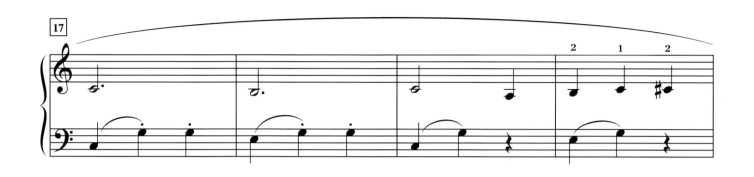

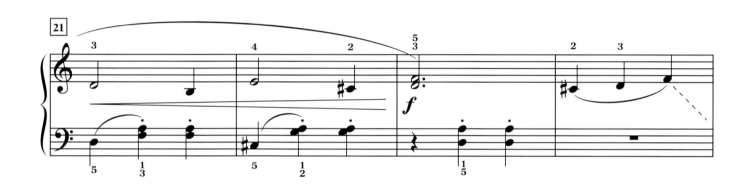

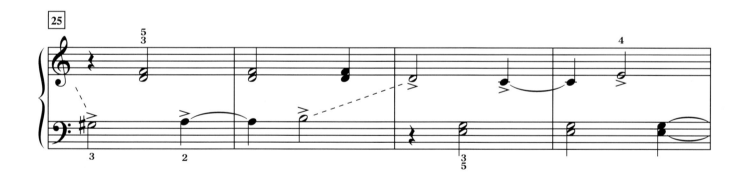

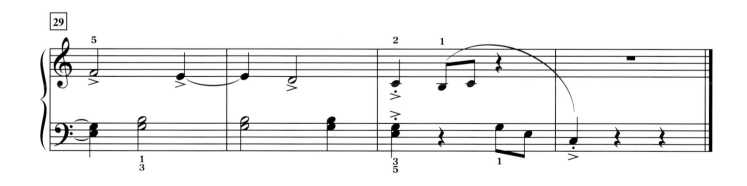

The Nutcracker

A Dramatic Ballet in Two Acts

Composer: **Peter Ilyich Tchaikovsky**

Story: **Based on a story by E. T. A. Hoffmann**

First performed: **1892 in St. Petersburg, Russia**

The Story

There is an exciting Christmas party at Clara's house! It is Christmas Eve, and everyone is dancing.
Clara and her brother Fritz are playing with their friends around the Christmas tree when Mr. Drosselmeyer, Clara's godfather, enters with gifts. He gives Clara a very special nutcracker in the shape of a soldier. She is thrilled! Because Fritz is jealous, he takes the nutcracker from Clara, but it slips through his hands and breaks. Clara is heartbroken, but Mr. Drosselmeyer repairs it, telling her the toy will be fine by morning. Clara puts the nutcracker in a little doll bed under the tree before going to sleep.

Later that night while everyone is asleep, Clara returns to the tree to see if her special gift is safe. As she approaches the tree, the clock chimes midnight. Suddenly, strange things start to happen! The tree begins to grow taller and taller. The Mouse King and his army of mice appear. The Nutcracker comes to life and gathers up an army of toy soldiers to fight the Mouse King. Although he is brave, the Nutcracker seems to be losing the battle. Clara throws her slipper at the Mouse King, who takes his army and runs away. Suddenly the Nutcracker turns into a handsome prince and invites Clara to go with him on a journey to enchanted lands.

They travel to the beautiful Land of Snow and then to the Kingdom of Sweets, where they are welcomed by the Sugarplum Fairy at her castle. They are entertained there by many dancers: Spanish, Arabian, Chinese and Russian. There are dancers with flutes and even a garden of dancing flowers. The Sugarplum Fairy reappears with her own prince, and they dance a final tribute to the guests.

Clara wakes up in her own bed on Christmas morning, wondering if this had all been a dream.

About the Ballet

The Nutcracker is a ballet based on the story *The Nutcracker and the Mouse King,* by German storyteller E. T. A. Hoffmann. It is the only famous ballet in which a child plays the most important character. This two-act ballet was Tchaikovsky's third and final ballet.

When the ballet was first presented, it was not a success. The original choreographer, Marius Petipa (whom Tchaikovsky had worked closely with on *Swan Lake* and *The Sleeping Beauty*), had taken ill. Therefore, the ballet was choreographed by Petipa's assistant, Lev Ivanov. Much of the ballet was considered ineffective, giving few opportunities for the ballerina to show her ability. Since then, many choreographers have created their own successful versions of *The Nutcracker*.

The music for *The Nutcracker* is some of the most popular and recognized music ever composed. Many ballet companies perform *The Nutcracker* every Christmas, and numerous orchestras perform *The Nutcracker Suite*, a collection of eight pieces from the ballet, chosen by Tchaikovsky himself.

About the Composer

Russian composer Peter Ilyich Tchaikovsky (1840–1893) wrote piano music, concertos, symphonies and operas, but he is remembered best for his three ballets—*Swan Lake, The Sleeping Beauty* and *The Nutcracker*.

Even as a very young child, Tchaikovsky loved music. His parents encouraged him to develop his talent, but they did not encourage him to pursue music as a career. They wanted him to be a lawyer. He graduated from law school and worked for the government, but soon after, he enrolled in the St. Petersburg Conservatory to study music seriously. He wrote a letter to his sister, saying that while he didn't think he would become a famous musician, he still felt he must work in music because that is what he loved to do most.

About the Music: Dance of the Sugarplum Fairy (arrangement on pages 30–31)

Dance of the Sugarplum Fairy is a solo at the beginning of the second act, when Clara and the prince arrive in the Kingdom of Sweets.

For *The Nutcracker*, Tchaikovsky used a celesta, a brand new keyboard instrument that he discovered in Paris. He had one secretly sent to him so he could be the first to use it in Russia. The celesta's tinkling tones are heard in *Dance of the Sugarplum Fairy*.

The Nutcracker Cross Word

Complete the sentences below, then write the answers in the crossword puzzle. Choose your answers from the given words.

| CELESTA |
| CHRISTMAS |
| FRITZ |
| GODFATHER |
| HOFFMANN |
| NUTCRACKER |
| PRINCE |
| SLIPPER |
| SOLDIERS |
| SUGARPLUM |
| SWEETS |

ACROSS

1. *The Nutcracker* is based on a story by E. T. A. _____ .
4. Tchaikovsky had a new keyboard instrument called a _____ secretly sent to him to use in this ballet.
6. Clara and the prince are welcomed by the _____ Fairy at her castle.
7. Clara throws her _____ at the Mouse King and scares him away.
9. The story takes place on _____ Eve.
10. The nutcracker gathers an army of toy _____ to fight the Mouse King.

DOWN

2. Mr. Drosselmeyer is Clara's _____.
3. Clara receives a special _____ as a gift.
5. _____ accidentally breaks Clara's gift.
6. The prince and Clara travel to the Land of Snow and the Kingdom of _____.
8. The nutcracker turns into a handsome _____.

Dance of the Sugarplum Fairy*

(from *The Nutcracker*)

Peter Ilyich Tchaikovsky
Arr. Margaret Goldston

---

* Arrangements of other pieces from *The Nutcracker* can be found in Margaret Goldston's *A Simply Classic Nutcracker* (18077).

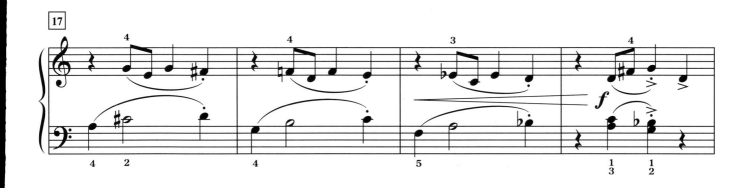

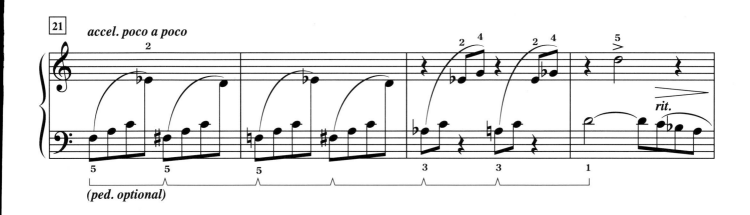

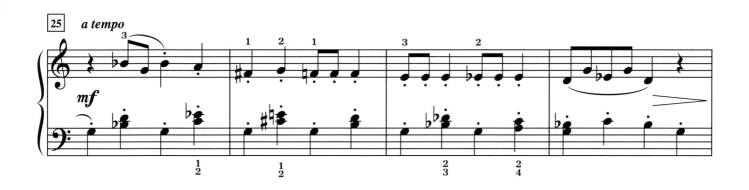

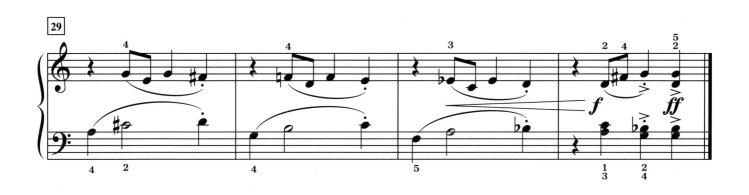

La Gioconda

A Dramatic Opera in Four Acts

Composer: **Amilcare Ponchielli**

Story: **Based on a tale by Victor Hugo**

First performed: **1876 in Milan, Italy**

The Story

The story begins on a beautiful spring day in the Italian seaport of Venice. Gioconda and her blind mother are attending the city festival. Gioconda is a good woman who earns money to take care of her beloved mother by singing in the public squares. She is "the ballad[1] singer" (the meaning of the Italian words "la gioconda"). Barnaba, an evil spy, is watching Gioconda. He is in love with her, but she has no interest in him. She is in love with a man named Enzo, a prince disguised as a sea captain. Although Enzo likes Gioconda, he is truly in love with Laura, who is the wife of Alvise, one of the high government officials. At one time, Laura and Enzo were engaged to be married, but were unfortunately separated, and Laura was forced to marry Alvise. Laura and Enzo have found each other again in this city.

Barnaba is jealous and angry because Gioconda loves Enzo, so he carries out a plan to have Enzo put in prison. Gioconda promises Barnaba that she will marry him if only he will free Enzo. Barnaba agrees, and Enzo is freed.

Alvise wants to kill Laura because he finds out she still wants to marry Enzo. Gioconda learns of this and knows that Laura's life is in danger. Because of her love for Enzo and her desire to see him happy, Gioconda rescues Laura and helps Laura and Enzo escape together on a ship.

With Enzo gone, Barnaba searches for Gioconda to make her his bride. When he comes to her door, she kills herself so she will not have to marry him. With a cry of anger, he rushes away from her lifeless body.

---

[1] A ballad is a simple, narrative song.

About the Ballet

La Gioconda is not actually a ballet, but rather a four-act opera that includes ballet. Ballet was a very important part of the earliest operas, and every opera was expected to have a ballet included in the production.

The story is based on *Angelo, Tyrant of Padua*, a tale by Victor Hugo (a famous French poet and novelist). The dramatic plot, which takes place in 17th-century Italy, incorporates feelings of love, hate, jealousy, revenge and sacrifice.

Dance of the Hours, the most familiar music from *La Gioconda*, is a large ballet number. This music was used in Walt Disney's animated feature film *Fantasia* (1940) and was also turned into a humorous camp song called *Hello Muddah, Hello Faddah* (1963) by Allan Sherman.

About the Composer

Giacomo Puccini (pictured above) studied with Amilcare Ponchielli at the Milan Conservatory.

Italian composer Amilcare Ponchielli (1834–1886) is mostly known as a composer of opera. He studied music at the Milan Conservatory and wrote his first opera soon after graduation. Later in life, he taught composition at the Milan Conservatory where he was the teacher of the great opera composer, Giacomo Puccini. The opera *La Gioconda* (often called his masterpiece) is Ponchielli's best-known work. Its strong melodies and sense of drama established him as a potential successor to the great opera composer Giuseppe Verdi. However, Ponchielli died before he could fulfill that destiny.

About the Music: Dance of the Hours (arrangement on pages 36–37)

Dance of the Hours is performed in Act III during a scene that takes place in a big hall in Alvise's house. The use of various lighting effects, costume changes and choreography help depict the hours of dawn, daylight, evening and night.

La Gioconda

Using the code at the bottom of the page, fill in the blanks.

La Gioconda means

"___ ___ ___   ___ ___ ___ ___ ___ ___   ___ ___ ___ ___ ___ ___."
20 8 5   2 1 12 12 1 4   19 9 14 7 5 18

It is not actually a ballet, but an ___ ___ ___ ___ ___ .
15 16 5 18 1

It was composed by

___ ___ ___ ___ ___ ___ ___ ___   ___ ___ ___ ___ ___ ___ ___ ___ ___ .
1 13 9 12 3 1 18 5   16 15 14 3 8 9 5 12 12 9

In the story, the evil Barnaba loves ___ ___ ___ ___ ___ ___ ___ ___ ,
7 9 15 3 15 14 4 1

but she loves ___ ___ ___ ___ .
5 14 26 15

The famous ballet number from this opera is

___ ___ ___ ___ ___   ___ ___   ___ ___ ___   ___ ___ ___ ___ ___ .
4 1 14 3 5   15 6   20 8 5   8 15 21 18 19

NUMBER CODE:

A	1	N	14
B	2	O	15
C	3	P	16
D	4	Q	17
E	5	R	18
F	6	S	19
G	7	T	20
H	8	U	21
I	9	V	22
J	10	W	23
K	11	X	24
L	12	Y	25
M	13	Z	26

Gondolas in Venice

Dance of the Hours

(from *La Gionconda*)

Amilcare Ponchielli
Arr. Margaret Goldston

Gaîté Parisienne

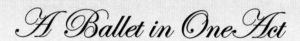

A Ballet in One Act

Composer: **Jacques Offenbach**

Story: **Based on a story by Etienne de Beaumont**

First performed: **1938 in Monte Carlo, Monaco**

The Story

In one of the most popular restaurants in Paris, waiters and cleaning girls are getting the restaurant ready for the evening. The waiters are dancing comically to amuse the girls. A girl who sells flowers enters the restaurant and gives each waiter a bouquet. She joins the waiters in a dance, then sets up her tray of flowers to sell.

Then the beautiful glove seller enters. All the men gather around her and insist that she dance with them. Everyone is watching her dance when the Peruvian, a newcomer on vacation in Paris, enters the restaurant. He is excited and happy to be there. First he goes to the flower girl, but then notices the beautiful glove seller.

The Baron enters. The flower girl thinks he is handsome and she goes to him, but the Baron ignores her because he has seen the glove seller. The Baron and the glove seller move towards each other and begin to dance a romantic waltz.

Five soldiers and an officer enter. Shortly thereafter, everyone in the restaurant is surprised by the entrance of La Lionne, the popular beauty of Paris. She is accompanied by the Duke, but is immediately attracted to the officer. The restaurant becomes very lively with even more dancing as the can-can dancers enter with their dance master. All the guests gather together to watch these dancers line up and display their high kicks. When the dance master commands, the can-can girls all fall to the floor in splits. This excites the crowd even more, and they all join in the dance.

When the dancing finally comes to a close, the music becomes soft, and the couples start to leave together: the Baron with the glove seller, the flower girl with the Duke and La Lionne with the officer. The Peruvian remains alone as all the couples wave goodbye.

About the Ballet

Gaîté Parisienne[1] ("The Gay Parisian") is a one-act ballet based on a story by Etienne de Beaumont, who also designed the scenery and costumes. The entire ballet takes place in one setting–a 19th-century Paris restaurant where people come to eat, drink, dance and find romance. The unusual thing about *Gaîté Parisienne* is that the ballet was created 58 years after the death of the composer, using music he had written for other settings.

The Paris Opera House, c. 1868

About the Composer

Jacques Offenbach (1819–1880), whose real name was Jacob Eberst, was born in Germany. His father, Isaac, was from the little German town of Offenbach. When the family moved to Cologne, Germany, Isaac wanted everyone to know where he was from, so he changed the family name to Offenbach.

A cellist, Jacques moved to Paris when he was 14 and got a job playing in the orchestra at the Opera House. He then became a soloist and toured Europe. In 1855, he opened a theater in Paris to present short, humorous musical shows. At that time, he also began composing music for his own shows. One of these, *King Carrot*, had a chorus of people dressed as vegetables!

Offenbach wrote 97 operettas and one opera. His most popular pieces are *Can-Can* and *Barcarolle*, both of which are used in *Gaîté Parisienne*.

Toulouse-Lautrec poster featuring Can-Can dancing

About the Music: Can-Can

(arrangement on pages 42–43)

The can-can was a lively dance that became popular in Paris in the mid-1800s. It is known for its use of high kicking steps. Offenbach's composition *Can-Can* first appeared in the operetta *Orpheus in the Underworld*, which was first performed in 1861. It is now probably the most famous piece of music he ever composed. In *Gaîté Parisienne*, the *Can-Can* is performed towards the end of the story, creating the height of the excitement.

---

[1] pronounced "gay-TAY pah-ree-zee-EHN"

The Gaîté Parisienne  Game

Draw a line to the correct name.

The composer

He is on vacation in Paris

A show with a chorus dressed as vegetables

She leaves the restaurant with the Baron

Offenbach's real name

Leaves the restaurant with the Duke

The popular beauty of Paris

King Carrot

Offenbach

La Lionne

the Peruvian

Jacob Eberst

the glove seller

the flower girl

Can-Can

(from *Gaîté Parisienne*)

Jacques Offenbach
Arr. Margaret Goldston

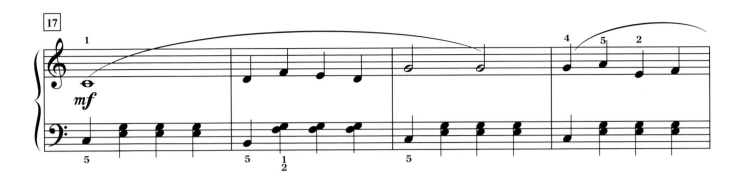

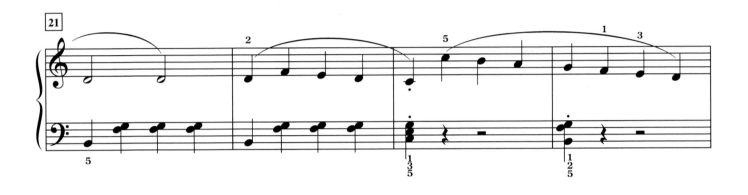

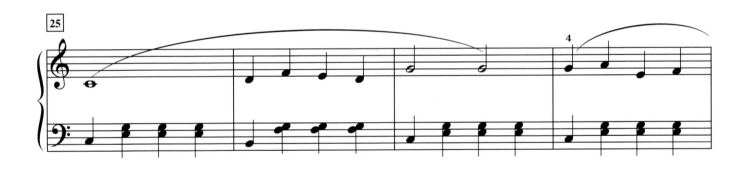

Les Sylphides

A "Ballet Blanc" in One Act

Composer: **Frédéric François Chopin**

Story: **Not based on a story**

First performed: **1909 in Paris, France**

The Story

This ballet does not have a story line, although the dances suggest a romance by the moonlight.

The dancing takes place in a forest near an old, deserted churchyard, late at night. The female dancers represent the spirits of young girls who have died. They are dressed in white, filmy costumes as they dance by the light of the moon. One male dancer (dressed in white tights, white shirt and a black vest) dances with the young girls.

As the curtain rises, the dancers are seen in an opening group, with the one male dancer supporting two of the leading ballerinas. The action of the ballet is a series of dances set to music by Frédéric François Chopin.

The dances vary according to the style of each piece and include two mazurkas, one nocturne, one prelude and three waltzes. The ballet ends with the entire corps dancing to the *Grand Waltz*.

Les Sylphides
(New York, 1916)

About the Ballet

Les Sylphides[1] is French for "the spirits." It is a one-act *ballet blanc* (meaning "white ballet") in which the female dancers all wear long, delicate white costumes. The famous Russian choreographer, Michel Fokine, wanted to create a ballet to show how expressive dance could be without a story. He created the ballet in 1908 for his students at the Imperial Ballet School in St. Petersburg, Russia.

The music was not originally created for the ballet. Instead, the ballet features orchestrated versions of piano music by the great composer Frédéric François Chopin. In fact, the ballet was originally titled *Chopiniana*.

About the Composer

Frédéric François Chopin (1810–1849) was born near Warsaw, Poland. As a young man he moved to Paris, but he always loved his native Poland, which inspired much of his music. Chopin was a great pianist and composer who helped make the piano a popular solo instrument. He is well known for his many keyboard works, including the following types used in *Les Sylphides:*

mazurka—a Polish folk dance in triple meter (three beats to a measure). The tempo can range from slow to lively. It often has an accent on the third beat.

nocturne—means "night piece." The nocturne has a dreamy, romantic feeling. It generally has a song-like melody over a flowing, broken-chord accompaniment.

prelude—a short one-movement piece that contains a single theme (or musical idea).

waltz—a dance in triple meter, usually with a slow to moderate tempo. When written for piano, the waltz often has a lyrical right-hand melody with an "oom-pah-pah" left-hand chordal accompaniment.

About the Music: Grand Waltz, Op. 18 (arrangement on pages 48–49)

Often called the *Grand Valse Brilliante,* this waltz is used as the final dance number in *Les Sylphides.* All the performers are on stage, using swift, fluttering movements resembling butterfly wings.

---

[1] pronounced "lay sil-FEED"

Les Sylphides
"Tree"mendous MATCHING Game

Draw a line connecting the information below to the correct tree in the forest.
(Hint: You can find the descriptions for mazurka, nocturne, prelude and waltz in the
About the Composer section for Les Sylphides.)

1. **A Polish folk dance in triple meter**

2. **A short one-movement piece that contains a single theme**

3. **"Night piece"**

4. **A dance in triple meter, with a slow to moderate tempo**

5. **Has a dreamy, romantic feeling**

6. **Often has an accent on the third beat**

7. **Has a flowing, broken-chord accompaniment**

8. **Has an "oom-pah-pah" left-hand chordal accompaniment**

Grand Waltz

(from *Les Sylphides*)

Frédéric François Chopin
Op. 18
Arr. Margaret Goldston

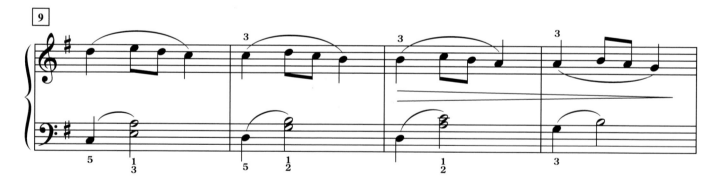

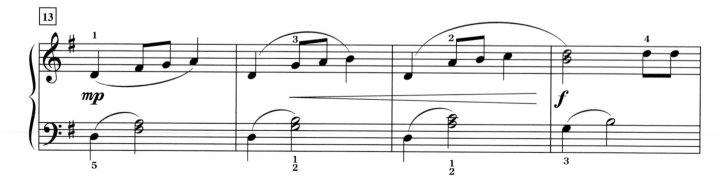

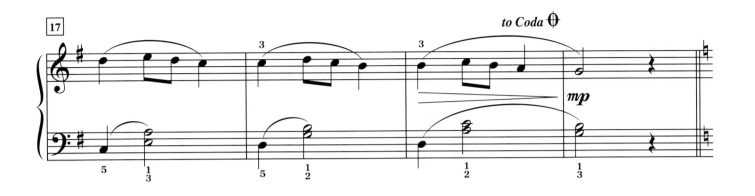

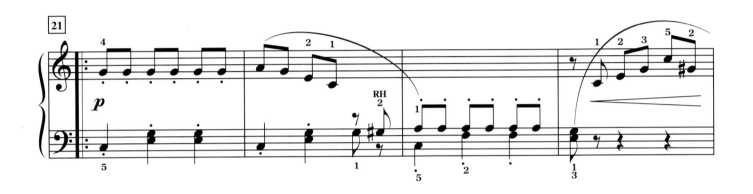

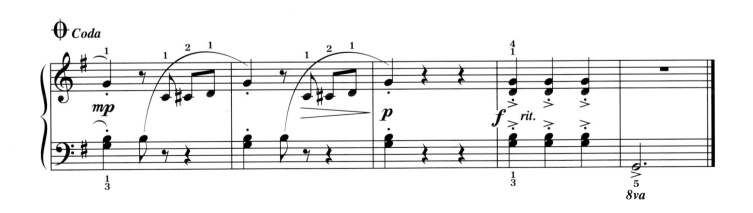

Coppélia

A Comic Ballet in Three Acts

Composer: **Léo Delibes**

Story: **Inspired by a story by E. T. A. Hoffmann**
Written by Charles Nuitter and Arthur Saint-Léon

First performed: **1870 in Paris, France**

The Story

This is the story of an old inventor named Dr. Coppélius, his daughter Coppélia and a young couple, Swanilda and Franz, who are to be married. Every day, Coppélia sits by her upstairs window reading, but never moves or speaks. One day, Franz is throwing kisses to Coppélia. Swanilda sees this and becomes very upset.

That evening, Swanilda finds a house key that was accidentally dropped by Dr. Coppélius. She and her friends decide to sneak in and see Coppélia. Just as they go into the house, Franz, who has his own plans to visit Coppélia, sneaks upstairs using a ladder from outside.

Inside the house, Swanilda and her friends explore Dr. Coppélius's workshop. They discover Coppélia sitting behind a curtain and realize that she is really just a doll! In fact, the workshop is filled with many mechanical dolls. Suddenly, Dr. Coppélius returns home and chases everyone away except for Swanilda, who has hidden behind Coppélia's curtain. Then Dr. Coppélius catches Franz climbing in through the window. Franz explains that he wants to marry Coppélia, unaware that she is a doll.

Giuseppina Bozzacchi in Coppélia
(Opéra, Paris, 1870)

Dr. Coppélius gets an idea. He has Franz drink a magic potion that causes him to fall asleep. He plans to magically take the life out of Franz's body and give it to Coppélia. After reciting some magic spells, Dr. Coppélius watches as Coppélia comes to life. He doesn't realize that Swanilda has put on the doll's dress and is pretending to be Coppélia. Swanilda, hoping to save Franz's life, dances and makes lots of noise to try to wake him. Finally, she pulls Franz to his feet, waking him up, and together they run out of the house to safety. Dr. Coppélius spots the doll lying on the floor and realizes that she never came to life after all.

The next day, Swanilda and Franz are married.

About the Ballet

In Coppélia, *a ballerina performs "doll" pantomine (stiff legs, angular hands).*

Coppélia, the story of a doll that comes to life, is a comic ballet in three acts. The story was inspired by a tale from the German storyteller E. T. A. Hoffmann (who also wrote *The Nutcracker*) and was written by Charles Nuitter and Arthur Saint-Léon. Saint-Léon also choreographed the ballet. *Coppélia* is sometimes referred to by its subtitle, *The Girl with the Enamel Eyes.*

The search for a ballerina to dance the part of Swanilda lasted three years. Eventually, a 16-year-old who had never danced in public won the part, after the original ballerina sprained her foot and could not dance.

When this ballet was first created, the use of male dancers was not very popular. Men were used on stage only to carry women. For many years, the role of Franz was danced by a woman disguised as a man.

In this ballet, many dancers pretend to be dolls that have been created by Dr. Coppélius. The dancers must be able to stand still for a long time so that their movements are a complete surprise to the audience.

About the Composer

Clement Philibert Léo Delibes (1836–1891), called "Léo," was born in France. Known as the first great composer of ballet music, Delibes was the first to unite the music with the choreography. He studied composition at the Paris Conservatory, later becoming a church organist, chorus master for the Paris Opéra and professor of composition at the Paris Conservatory. He composed both opera and ballet music. The music of Delibes inspired Tchaikovsky to write for the ballet. Delibes is mostly remembered for his music for the ballets *Coppélia* and *Sylvia,* and for his opera *Lakmé.*

About the Music: Mazurka (arrangement on pages 54–55)

During a trip to Eastern Europe, Delibes discovered many local folk tunes and rhythms, which he later used in *Coppélia.* The mazurka is a Polish folk dance with three beats in a measure. In *Coppélia,* the *Mazurka* is lively. It is danced in the first act by Swanilda, Franz and their friends in the town square, outside the house of Dr. Coppélius.

Coppélia Scramble

Unscramble the letters to spell words that complete each sentence.

1. *Coppélia* is the story of a _____ **(OLDL)** that comes to life.

2. The music was composed by _____ **(SEBLEID)**.

3. This ballet is sometimes called "The Girl with the _____ **(LEEMAN)** Eyes."

4. The _____ **(KRUMAAZ)** is a Polish folk dance with three beats

   in a measure.

5. *Coppélia* is a comic ballet in _____ **(HTERE)** acts.

6. At the end of the story, _____ **(DLAWISNA)** and

   _____ **(RZFNA)** are married.

7. Inside the house of Dr. Coppélius, Swanilda

   pretends to be _____

   (POPCILAÉ).

Czardas dancers (Paris, 1870). This national dance of Hungary was first introduced in ballet as a character dance in the first act of Coppélia.

Mazurka

(from *Coppélia*)

Léo Delibes
Arr. Margaret Goldston

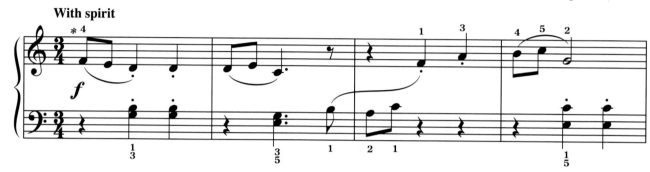

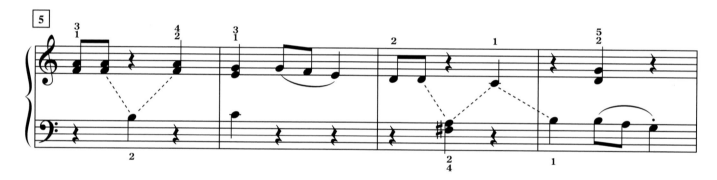

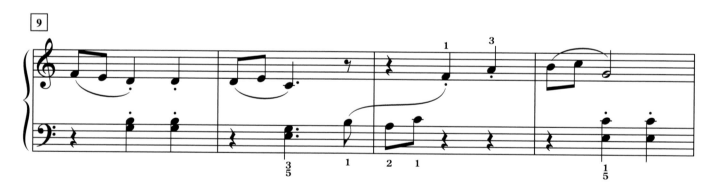

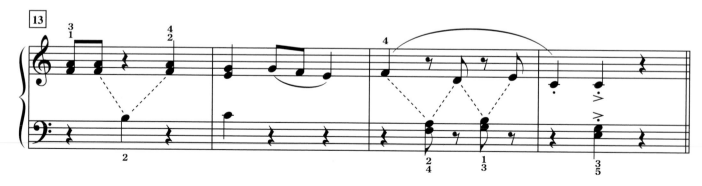

*Throughout the piece, ♩♪ can be played as ♩.♪ as originally written by Delibes.

Glossary of Ballet Terms

Arabesque ("ar-uh-BEHSK") A pose in which one leg is extended either in front or behind the dancer.

Ballare ("bahl-LAH-ray") To dance.

Ballerina One of the very best female dancers in a ballet company.

Ballet A performance of a dance group with music, costumes and scenery. It is performed without singing or spoken word and usually tells a story.

Ballet master/mistress The person who rehearses the ballet company and teaches the class.

Barre ("bar") A wooden hand rail attached to the dance studio wall. It is used by dancers to help them balance while exercising.

Choreography ("core-ee-AHG-ruh-fee") A pattern of steps in a dance. A *choreographer* is the person who arranges the steps.

Corps de ballet ("core de bal-LAY") The dancers in a ballet company who perform together in a group.

Danseur ("dahn-SUR") A male dancer.

Échappé ("ay-sha-PAY") A jump in which the feet begin closed, then open while in the air.

En pointe ("ahn point") Dancing up on the tips of the toes.

Jeté ("zheh-TAY") A jump from one foot to the other that uses a throwing motion of the body.

Leotard A skintight outfit worn for ballet class.

Mime The use of hand and arm gestures in ballet to help communicate the story.

Modern dance A blending of styles such as jazz, ethnic and folk dance, rock, tap, gymnastics and acrobatics. Dancers may have bare feet; costumes can be anything that helps express the dance.

Pas de deux ("pah de duh") A dance for two people.

Relevé ("rul-luh-VAY") Lifting the heels off the floor and raising the body.

Turnout A basic dance technique in which the legs are turned outward by having the knees turned away from each other.

Variation A solo dance with a series of difficult movements.